SARAH
AND
THE MAGIC PIANO

Story
Mike Biskup with Kurt Erickson

Music
Kurt Erickson

Art
Mike Biskup

Musical Engraving
BCP Music

First Edition
Patent Pending
Copyright © 2017 SoundtracksYouPlay

This material may not be photocopied, reproduced, or stored in any form or by any means without the prior permission of the author. All rights reserved.

For more information, products, games, gifts, etc. . .
visit: sarahandthemagicpiano.com

Greetings from Kurt Erickson and Mike Biskup!

Sarah and the Magic Piano is like nothing you've ever seen. It's an imaginative music storybook, a collection of 18 fun and evocative beginning piano pieces, a colorful and quirky animated video, and a separate play-along video where you perform the pieces to create the soundtrack in real time while the story is being read.

Playing the piano has never been so much fun!

Enjoy this book, and please visit **sarahandthemagicpiano.com** to check out the videos and create your very own Sarah experience.

Table Of Contents

Exploring Grandma Della Mae's House 7
Strange Contraptions and Unusual Instruments 9
Trouble Keeping the Band Together 10
Falling Leaves 13
The Final Acorn 15
The Earth and the Snail 17
The Mouse and the Train 19
Passing the Torch of Life 21
Bell Dance 23
Flea Fight! 25
Flea Circus 26
Mist 29
Big Storm's A-Comin'! 31
Sailing 33
Very Sneaky 35
Best Not to Ask 37
Baroque Dance 39
Benediction 41

Sarah Haverstock is ten years old. She likes to walk her dogs, make up stories with friends, and play the piano.

One day, Sarah and her mom went to visit Sarah's grandma, Della Mae, who lived in an old, creaky house in the center of town. After an hour or so of listening to her mom and grandma catch up on family news, Sarah snuck off to explore. She knew most of the old place very well, but there was one door at the end of a long, dimly lit hallway that she had never been through. The door was a deep, rich red color. Painted in the center was an eerie picture of a light bulb with a heart and a brain inside. This detailed image had always sent jitters through Sarah's veins and kept her from venturing in. Today, however, she was feeling brave so she decided to find out what was inside. She approached the door, grasped the old brass handle and opened it with a squeak. She started down a long set of cold concrete stairs into a dark, dank basement.

Sarah couldn't find a light switch, but the open door behind her allowed in just enough light to reveal a side of her grandma that Sarah had never known. As she crept through the dimly lit room, she spied dozens of strange contraptions, bizarre looking mechanical gadgets, and a workbench cluttered with tools. She also found a collection of unusual musical instruments, including a dusty piano unlike any she had seen before. The piano was adorned with a variety of colorful lights, which appeared to be salvaged from old cars, and a multitude of interesting looking knobs and switches of all types and sizes.

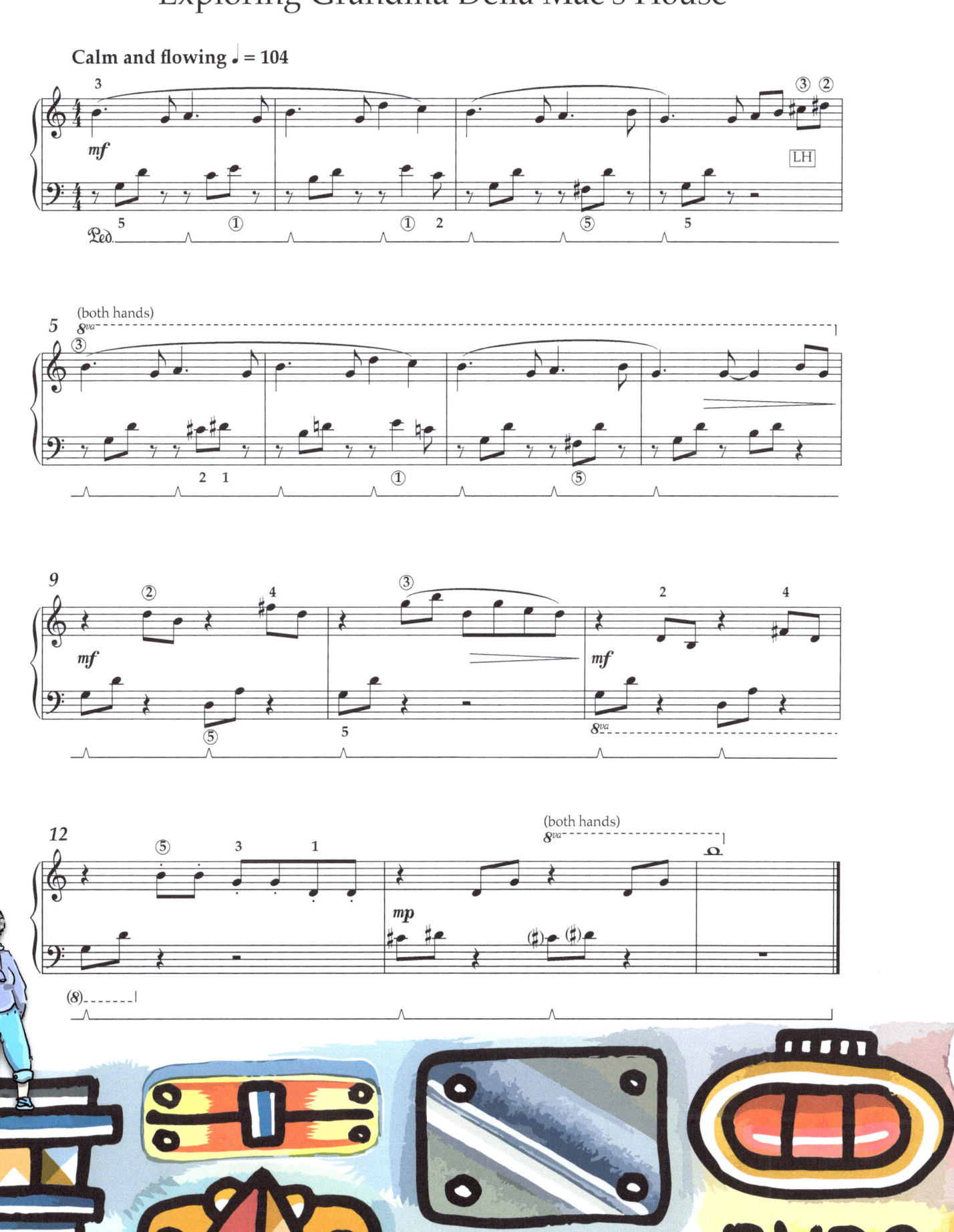

Sarah wondered to herself where all of these odd and interesting things had come from. On a shelf in the far corner of the basement, Sarah found a barely operational flashlight and a scrapbook of old photos and newspaper clippings, which began to put pieces of the mystery together.

The articles in the scrapbook chronicled her grandma's life as that of an ordinary housewife turned wildly successful inventor. The book revealed that she had designed dozens of useful household gadgets that earned her international acclaim and millions of dollars. Her most successful creation was the Radio Toaster, which gave people around the globe something to do while they waited for their toast to pop.

Further entries in the scrapbook revealed that at the peak of her career, she changed course from the ultra-practical, bread and butter world of household gadgets, to the uncharted realm of jazz ensemble size reduction, or "J.E.S.R." Her husband, the leader of a traveling jazz band, always had difficulties keeping his bands together due to personal differences exacerbated by long road trips in crowded vans. She decided that if she could lower the number of players needed in the band, she could relieve some of the stress of being on the road, thus improving the band's performances and stabilizing the personnel. She set out to combine various instruments that would allow one musician to play the parts of two. Her first attempt resulted in the Tubatar — a tuba/guitar combo which, although brilliant, was exceedingly difficult to play. Next came the Banjoboe. The musicians in the band were thankful for her concern for their welfare, but none could master the complexities of her new instruments. Disappointed, but not deterred, she set out to improve the design and functionality of a musical instrument that requires no musicians at all — the Playerless Piano.

Trouble Keeping the Band Together

Swing the 8th notes! (♫ = ♩♪) ♩ = 104

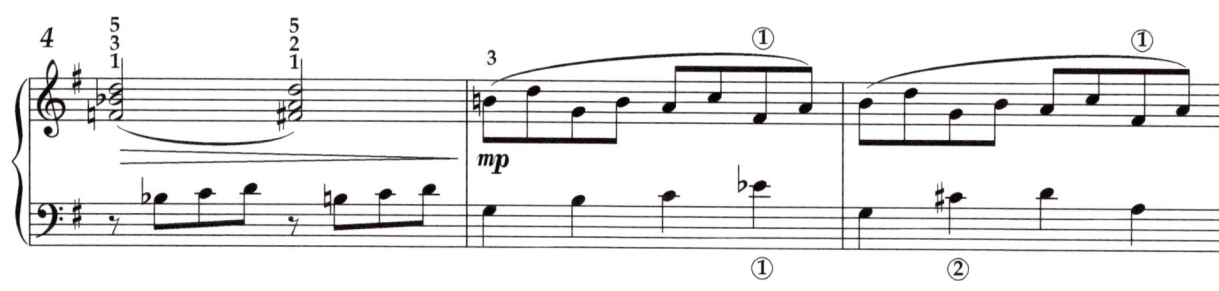

Suddenly, the door to the basement slammed shut. Sarah screamed, and the room was black. A dim, red light in the far corner of the room began pulsating. Faint musical notes played, which slowly grew louder and filled the room with beautiful whirling tones. More lights flickered and flashed, and soon Sarah could see that all the commotion was coming from the strange, old piano. Slowly the notes began to establish a rhythm as a swirling spectrum of color and sound erupted from this amazing instrument. Piercing lights shot through the room as fog rolled out on the floor toward Sarah's feet. One moment she was stiff with fear, and the next she was brimming with excitement. It was the most beautiful piece of music she had ever heard, and the most beautiful spectacle she had ever seen.

When the music finally came to an end and the light show began to subside, a single light remained and gave Sarah a good look at the amazing old piano. She studied it in awe. How had so much music and light suddenly sprung forth from her grandmother's creation? And why was this amazing invention just sitting in her basement where no one could experience it?

A book of sheet music resting on the music stand fluttered slightly, as if blowing in a breeze, and caught Sarah's eye. She cautiously approached the instrument. The book was called Sarah and the Magic Piano.

Sarah sat down on the bench, opened the book to the first piece of music, and waited for the amazing piano to begin its performance — but nothing happened. So she looked over the piece and began to play it herself. Sarah's fingers found the keys easily, and the simple tune filled the basement with cascading layers of notes strung together like a friendship bracelet. Then came the next big surprise of the day — the basement walls were becoming transparent, and Sarah started catching blurry glimpses of leaves and branches beyond the bricks. She stood up from the piano to investigate and magically found herself in a deep forest of moss covered trees and rocks. Soft, green grass grew underfoot and delicate ferns brushed her ankles. Somewhere off in the distance, she could hear the amazing piano continuing to play the first piece in the book.

Falling Leaves

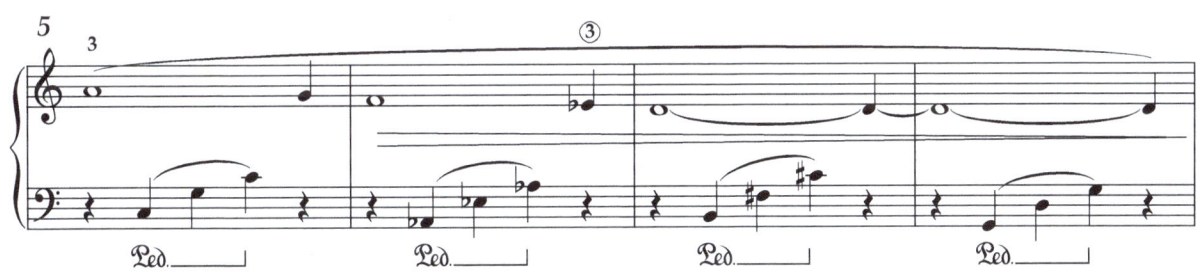

After walking through the forest for several minutes, she came to the edge of a large, sunny meadow with one giant, lone oak tree standing in the center. The oak's last few leaves were rustling in the autumn breeze and falling steadily to the ground. As one landed, the next began to fall, adding to a rich yellow carpet below.

A squirrel popped out of a hole in the ground and ran up the tree. Dashing from limb to limb, fearlessly clambering to the top, it grabbed an acorn in its mouth. Careening down, slipping and catching itself occasionally, the squirrel frantically but joyously ran down the tree and pounced to the ground. It darted into its hole with the acorn, deposited it on a pile, and dashed back out and up the tree for another. After several more trips, the squirrel plucked the final acorn from the oak. Surveying the meadow and the gray sky, it sniffed the air, perhaps getting a whiff of winter. It darted back down the tree, then into the hole, and gently curled up on a pile of acorns to rest.

 # The Final Acorn

Sarah wondered where the squirrel had gone and walked out into the meadow. As she neared his hole, she stopped quickly and retracted her foot, which had almost come down on top of a tiny, richly colored snail traversing a wild strawberry leaf. She bent down to get a closer look at the snail, which seemed to be growing larger. In fact, it *was* growing larger, and as she stood back up, the top of its shell reached her knee! Soon, the formerly tiny snail was the same size as the giant, lone oak.

Then Sarah somehow got an entirely different perspective. She was now watching the snail as if she were in outer space. The enormous creature had reached planetary proportions and was now slowly sliming along the earth, which was spinning on its heavenly axis. Stars twinkled in the blackness, surrounding the earth and the snail, and Sarah found herself in awe. Her trip to the her grandma's basement had become the adventure of a lifetime.

The sun rose over the snail's shell, and in the light Sarah saw a set of train tracks wrapped around it. A speeding train came into view from the backside of the shell, racing along the rails and furiously puffing gray and black smoke. Far ahead of the train, Sarah could see a tiny penny reflecting the sun as it lay on the tracks waiting to be flattened by the train's steel wheels. Then she noticed an extremely focused mouse running speedily alongside the train. It appeared to be a race. She looked back at the penny and saw a tear roll from Abe Lincoln's eye, over his cheek, and into his thick beard. As the pounding engine sped on, so too pounded the tiny heart of this extremely dedicated mouse, who seemed intent on saving Lincoln's life. Closer and closer and ever faster they raced. The train and the tracks rumbled like a pride of roaring lions. The engine's steel wheels were just inches from squashing Abe, when the tiny mouse pulled ahead slightly, jumped across the tracks, and nudged him off the rails to safety. The mouse, however, was not so lucky. He gave his life, sacrificed his future, to save a fellow creature in peril.

The Mouse and the Train

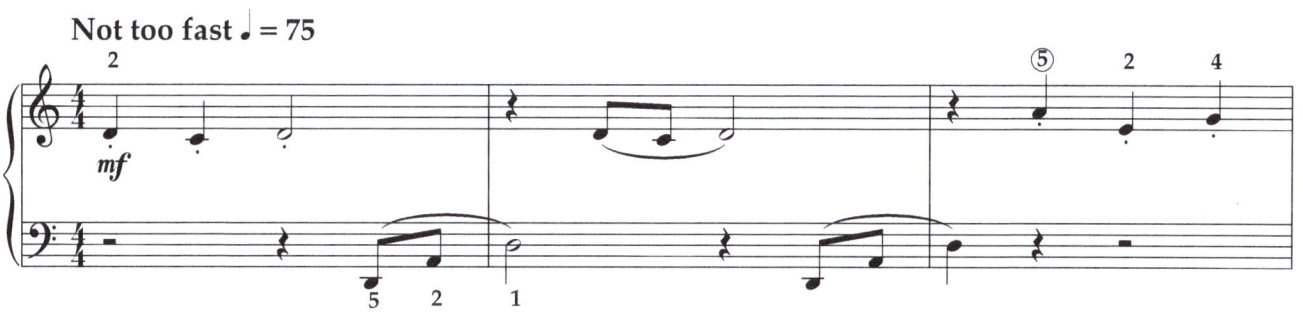

Sarah thought about the courageous mouse, then about the passing of the torch of life. She turned her attention to a long stone building which came into view after the train sped past, walked over to it, and peered in the open doorway. The Mouse was now lying unscathed, as if sleeping, on a wooden pedestal at the front of the building. Rays of colored light streamed in from stained glass windows high above, a candle burned, and smoke curled upward toward the vaulted stone ceiling.

Passing the Torch of Life

Slowly, gently, and with great feeling ♩ = 50

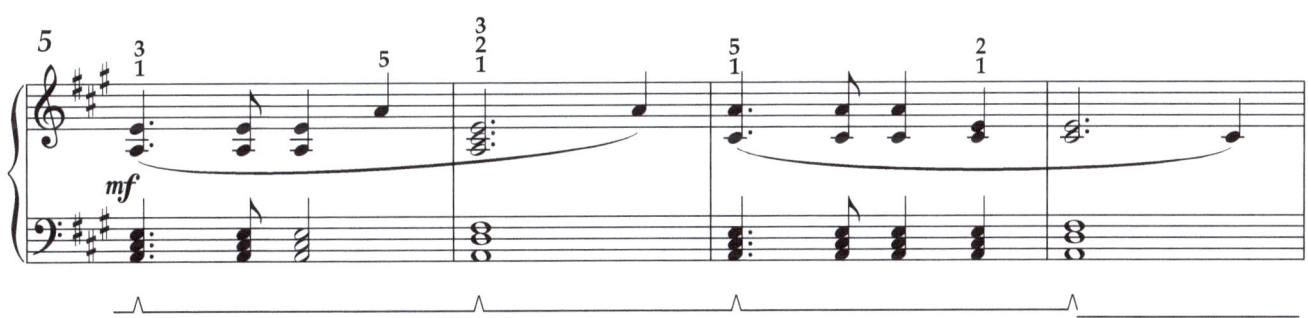

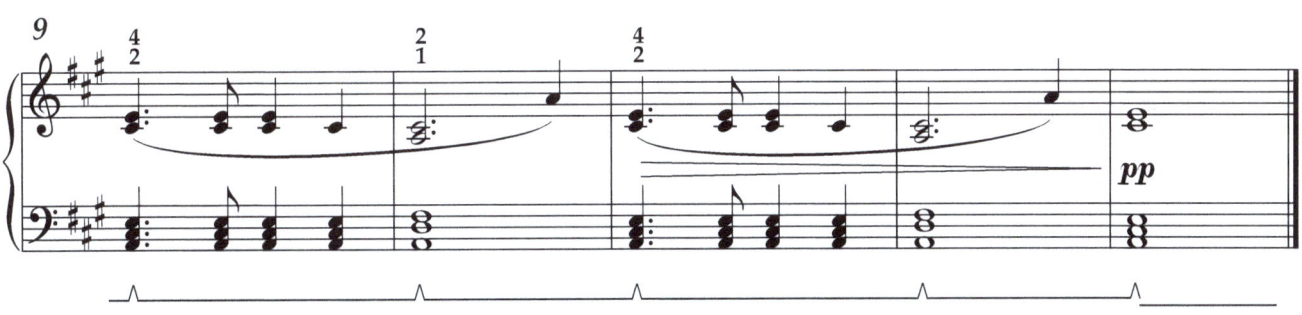

After a brief period of solemn reflection, Sarah walked in and looked more closely at the mouse. A ray of blue light fell on its side, clearly illuminating a patch of its silky soft, gray fur. As if magnified, the hairs began to be visible individually, and among them Sarah spotted a group of jubilant fleas. They were dancing a wonderful synchronous dance, twirling about their partners, laughing and singing with the music. Sarah would never have imagined all this activity could be taking place on the perished mouse's flank.

Bell Dance

Happy and dance-like ♩ = 100

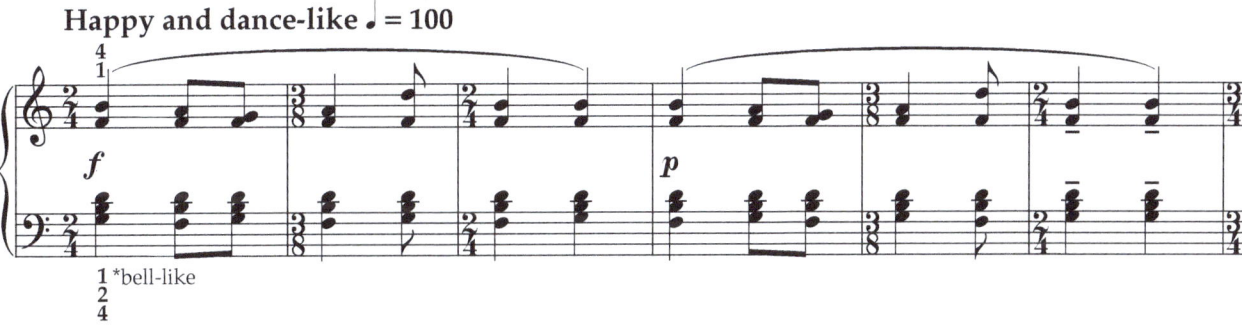

*bell-like

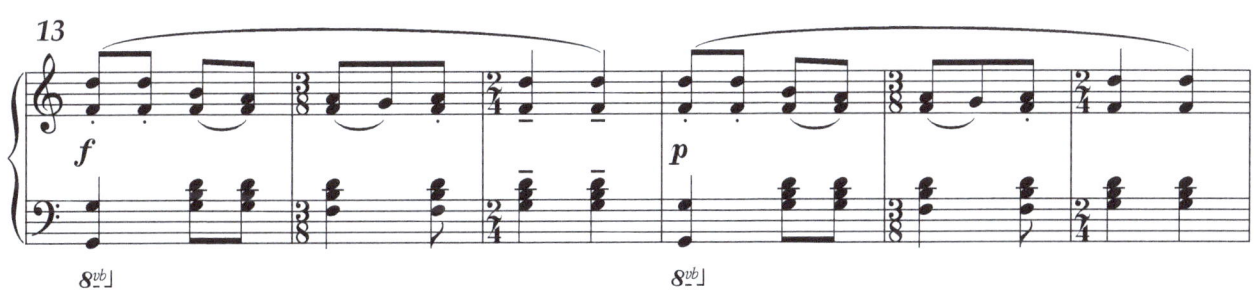

*To create a bell-like effect, hold pedal down for the entire piece.

As the music ended and the crowd of fleas began to clear the dance floor, a skirmish erupted. Two hot tempered fleas bumped each other as they went back to their seats. "Watch it buddy! I'll clean your clock," said one. "Please do. It's been looking a little dingy lately, kind of like your grandpa's false teeth," responded the second flea. "First I'll need a little soap," said the first, as he plucked a hair from the dead mouse's back to be used as a sword. "You couldn't clean your plate last night at dinner. What makes you think you'll do any better with me?" said the second, also plucking a sword, and assuming a very competent fencing stature. The crowd was shocked. "Such pointless aggression should be above you two," said one. "Yeah, you're acting like a couple of humans!" But the two fleas did not stop. The battle escalated and soon they were circling around, jabbing at each other with their swords. Their cursing and rude put-downs also escalated. The first flea, lunging wildly, slipped and lost his balance. He ended up on the floor with the second flea's sword at his neck. "Shall we dance?" asked the first. "How about a game of hopscotch?" replied the second.

Flea Fight!

The crowd erupted in laughter at the fantastic mock battle and moved onto the floor again, this time to play a variety of games. The fleas played hopscotch and tag, and some performed outstanding acrobatic feats. One juggled two grains of sand and a dust particle. Several others were playing with a length of string, jumping rope, then having a tiny tug of war. Finally, two fleas took the ends of the string and held them high, while another walked across the tightrope.

*This piece only contains notes that are always a half step away from each other. Use fingers 2 & 3 on ALL two note chords, and give fingers 1, 4, and 5 a well deserved holiday! Adventure Club - try playing low left hand notes with your elbow!

As this courageous flea walked graciously along, Sarah carefully studied the tightly pulled rope. Far beneath the braided surface, Sarah began to see the vastness of a deep, rocky canyon filling with mist.

Mist

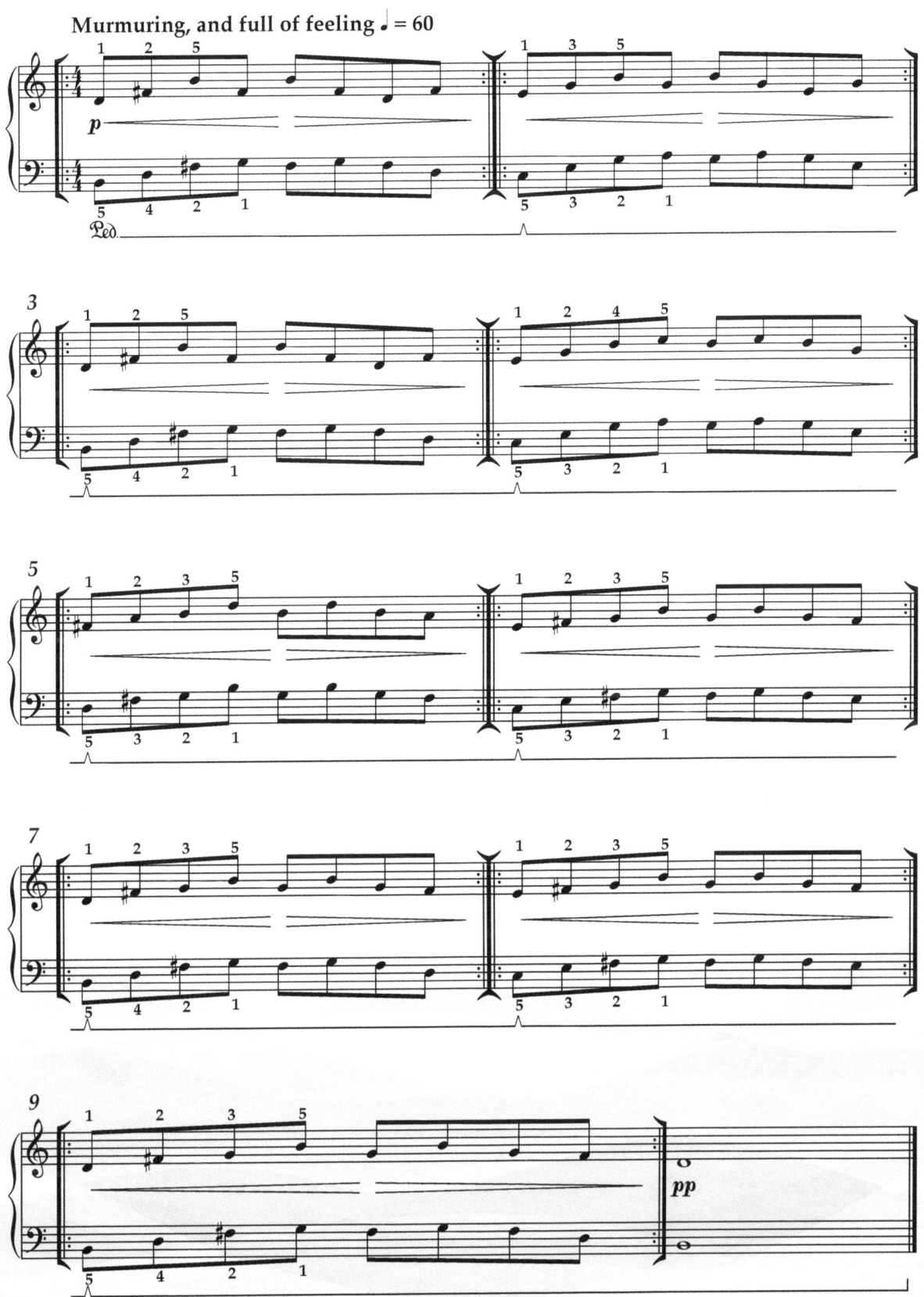

From beyond the distant mountains, a speckled gray and black bird soared into the canyon. As he flew, a magnificent storm spread out from beneath his enormous wings. Lightning flashed, thunder clapped, and rain came down in sheets. The precipitation rapidly filled the canyon with water and created a giant lake.

Big Storm's A'Comin'!

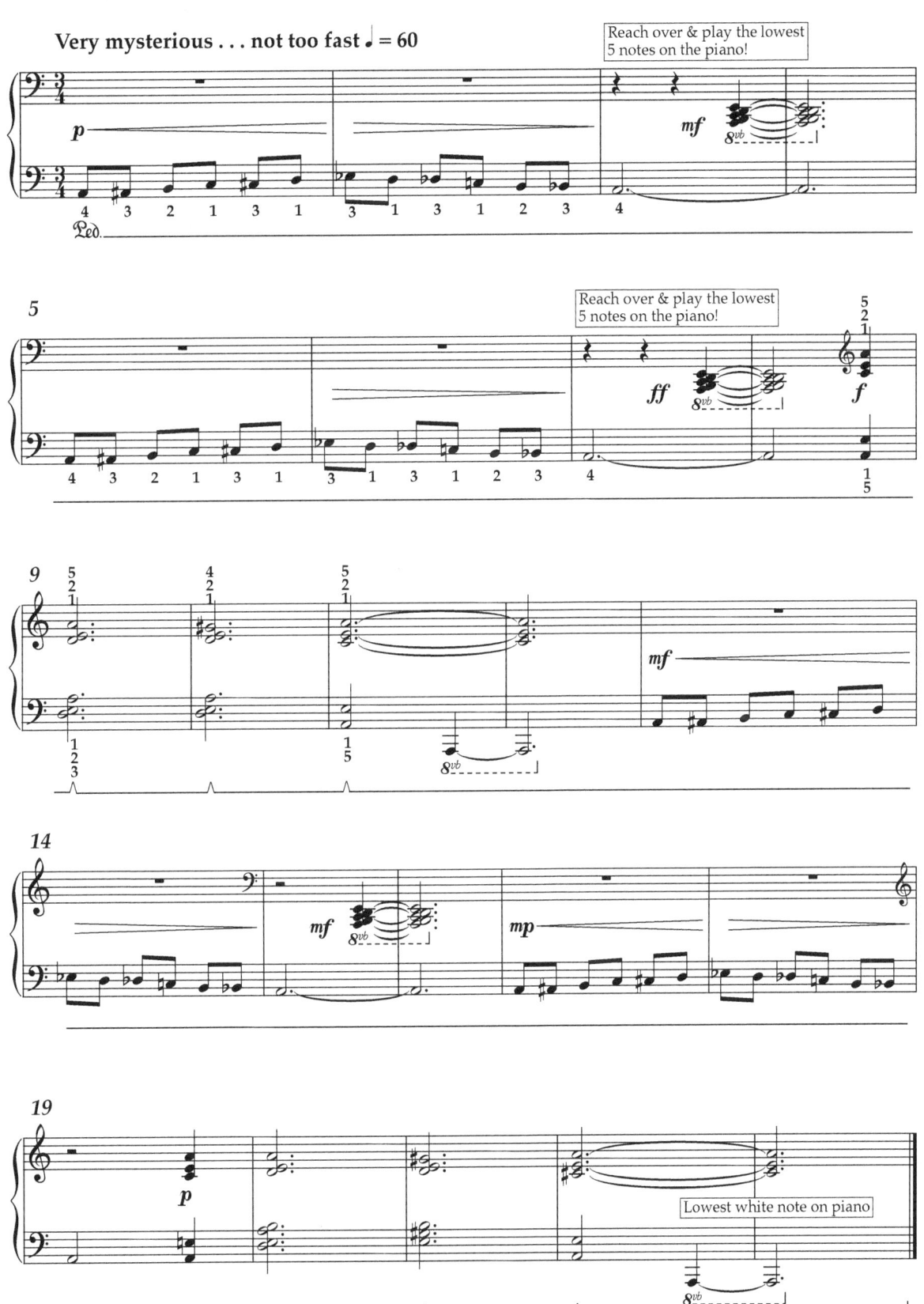

Then, just as quickly as the storm had started, it stopped, and the sun burst through a hole in the clouds. Every drop of water on every leaf of every tree glistened like a white flame. Sarah surveyed the beautiful lake that stretched out for miles and saw a small boat off in the distance. As it approached, she could see a gruff old, white-bearded sailor charting his course on a map blowing in the warm wind.

Sailing

The sailor docked his boat and came ashore. He sat down on one of two wooden crates, and began to tell a host of pointless stories. Sarah sat on the other crate listening and figured he must have spent a little too much time in the sun.

"*A young man is sneaking up on a mirror in his living room. He comes out of the closet, tiptoes behind a chair, then scoots behind the sofa and crawls under the rug. He slides on his belly to the wall under the mirror and takes a few deep breaths. He then jumps up in front of the mirror, screaming like an idiot, and scares himself back into the closet.*"

Very Sneaky

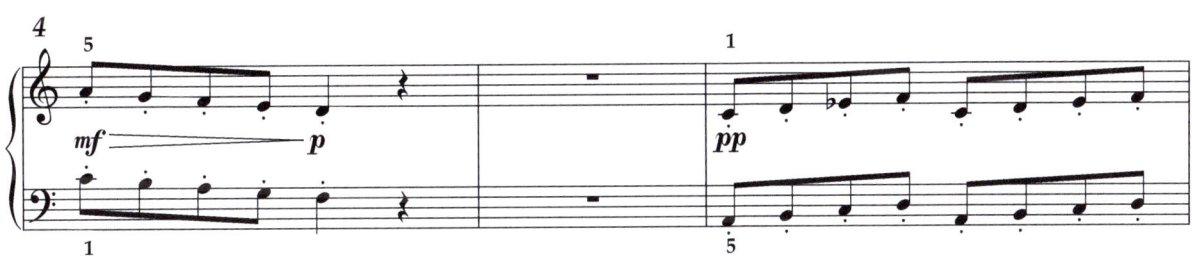
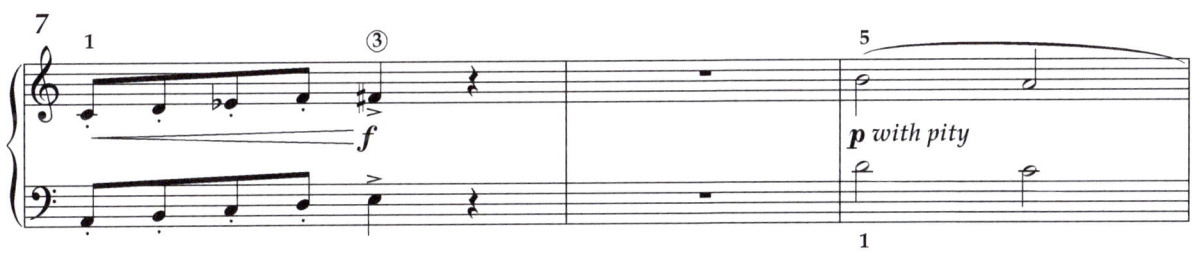
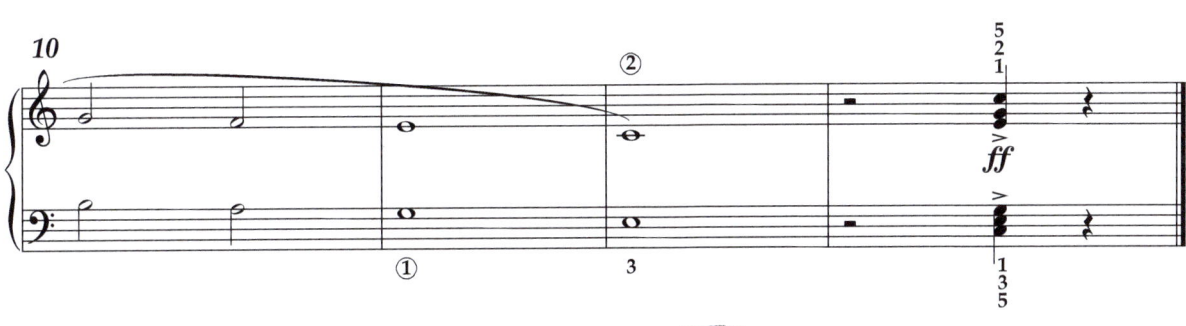

"Or... How about this one?"

"A penguin and a poodle share a dance in the back of a pickup being driven wildly over muddy country roads by a yak. The yak takes them into a small town with only two places of business: a Chinese restaurant and a fully automated, drive-through car wash. The yak buys the poodle some noodles and drives through the automated car wash while the penguin dances in the back. Now picture that!"

Best Not to Ask

A bit mysterious, and not too fast

"I heard this last one from my mother's mom."

"Three dynamic ballet dancers are leaping to and fro in a beautiful garden on top of a skyscraper. Music accompanies their masterful movements. One dives into a fish pond, comes up squirting water from her mouth like a fountain and proclaims, 'It takes more to be a good dancer than practice, practice, practice.' Another bounds up into the top of an apple tree, takes a bite out of a delicious red apple and says, 'A dance without emotion is like a kitchen without a fridge.' The last dancer runs full steam through the garden, across the entire top of the skyscraper, and leaps off the edge of the building. He lands in a passing helicopter next to a bewildered pilot who yells, 'What in the world were you thinking jumping off that building? You're fifty seven flights up!' "

Baroque Dance

Stately and proud

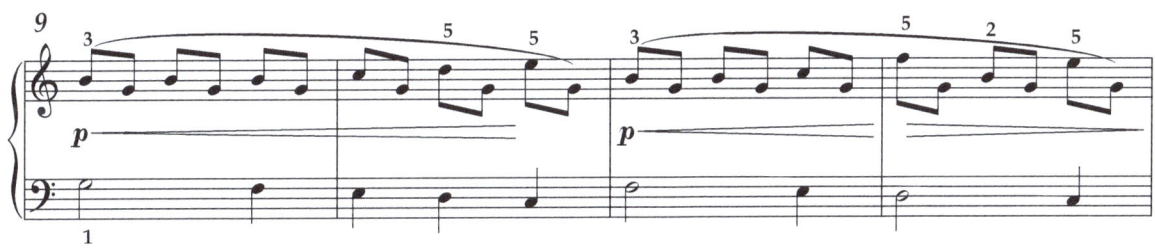
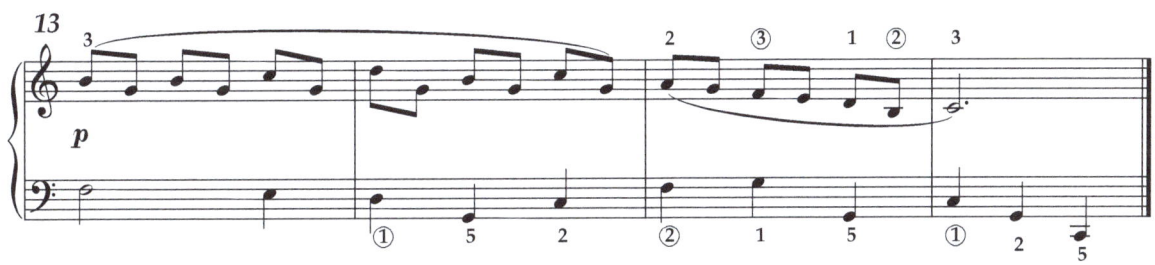

Sarah laughed at the insanity of the old fisherman's stories. She laughed so hard that she fell backwards off her crate and landed on the dock with a thud. As she picked herself up, she was once again in front of the playerless piano, which now appeared to be turning itself off. The lights dimmed again, the music stopped, and the fog cleared. The basement door opened, barely lighting the room from above. Sarah's grandma leaned in. "Sarah?" she called. Sarah jumped at the sound of the familiar voice. Then her grandmother flipped on a light, and Sarah scrambled up the stairs and into her arms. "That piano down there is incredible! I can't wait to tell you what happened!" Sarah said. "Oh, that old thing . . ." Grandma said. "I never had much luck with it, but I guess you had a different experience!"

The End.

Benediction

Not too fast; happy and fun

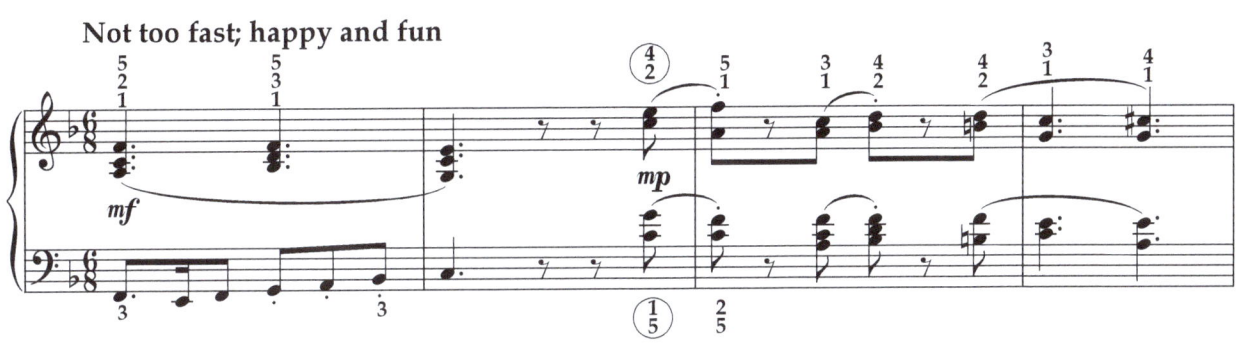
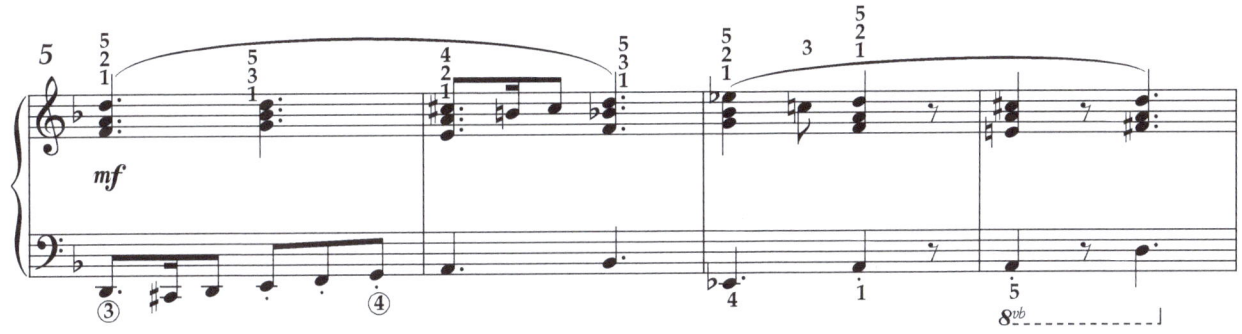

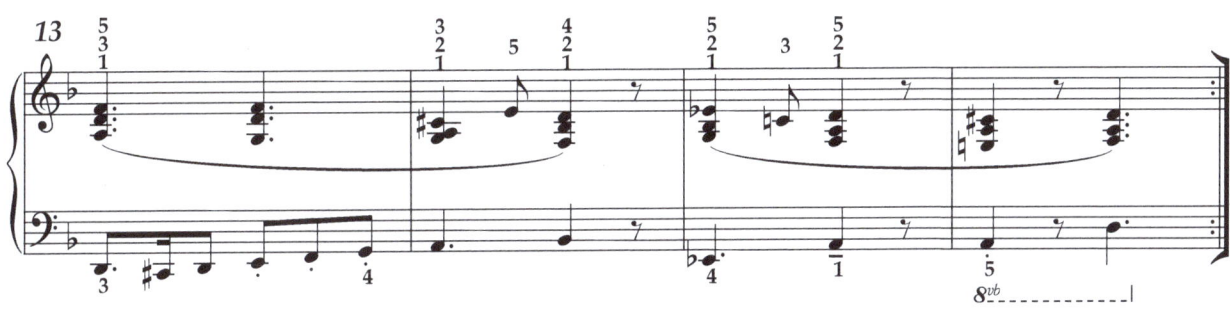

Kurt

Mike

Kurt and Mike met in school not long after these photos were taken...

Kurt Erickson, a critically acclaimed composer, grew up in Fresno, California in the Dark Ages before cell phones and the Internet, where he could be found spending countless hours at the piano, lost in the blissful raptures of Beethoven, boogie-woogie, and other assorted classical and not-so-classical music composers. Now residing in Northern California, he currently serves as composer-in-residence with San Francisco's LIEDER ALIVE! His works have been commissioned and performed by leading artists, including the late countertenor Brian Asawa, the Minnesota Orchestra, San Francisco Girls Chorus, Festival Opera, and San Francisco Opera's Ballet Master Lawrence Pech. While in his twenties, he served multi-year composer residencies at the Grace Cathedral and The National Shrine of Saint Francis of Assisi. He currently directs the Neue Lieder composer commissioning program, and has mentored young composers at music festivals, universities, and music conservatories. During the 2018-19 and 2019-20 seasons, a new soprano and orchestra song set will be performed domestically and internationally by a consortium of orchestras. He is a frequent performer with his wife, acclaimed soprano Heidi Moss Erickson. More about Kurt at www.kurterickson.com

Mike Biskup is an accomplished contemporary watercolorist whose subjects range from improvisational, imaginary landscapes to whimsical illustrations. Born in 1970 in Los Angeles, he comes from a family historically rich in artists, poets, and dreamers. As early as he can remember, he was voraciously drawing quirky dudes and funky hot rods with his two older brothers. He also cherished building contraptions, and telling tall tales. His paintings have long been featured in his adopted town of Port Townsend, Washington, and more recently in galleries in Seattle, Los Angeles, San Francisco, Boston, and more. His works can be found in the collection of Oscar-winning actress Patricia Arquette and many others around the world. As a singer-songwriter, he has penned over one hundred songs under his own name and with his brother, Tim, as "Big Butter." Mike's creativity is rooted in his belief that we humans, in all our diversity, are essentially interconnected, and with thoughtfulness can function together harmoniously. You'll often find Mike at home creating in his art/music studio, cooking with his three teenage children, growing vegetables in the family garden, or enjoying the company of his true love Laura. More about Mike at www.mikebiskup.com

www.ingramcontent.com/pod-product-compliance
Lightning Source LLC
Chambersburg PA
CBHW061400090426
42743CB00002B/81